LEGACIES

BLACK BRITISH PIONEERS

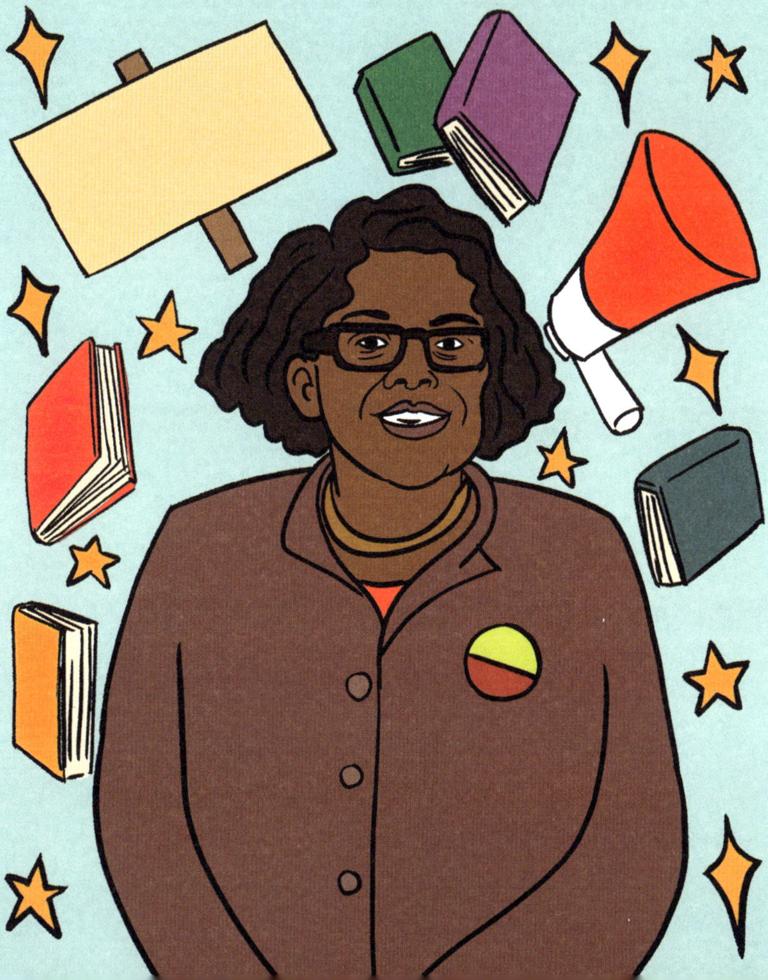

We are so thrilled that you are reading The Black Curriculum's first books! It means so much to us as a team, and I hope that these books inspire you to dive into your passions, hopes, and dreams. Go be great!

LAVINYA STENNETT, FOUNDER AND CEO OF THE BLACK CURRICULUM

The Black Curriculum is an organisation dedicated to promoting the learning of Black British history in and out of schools.

LEGACIES

BLACK BRITISH PIONEERS

WRITTEN BY
LANIA NARJEE

ILLUSTRATED BY
CHANTÉ TIMOTHY

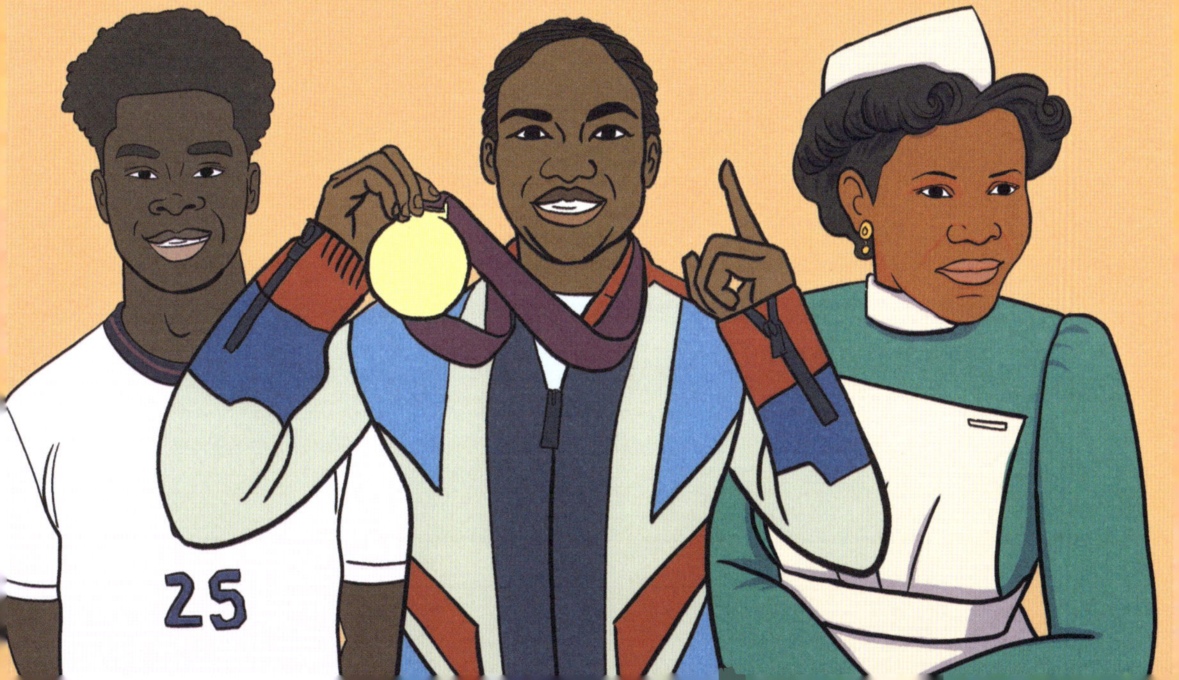

Contents

Timeline	6
Foreword	10
Introduction	12

CHAPTER 1: ARTISTS AND MUSICIANS

Early Jazz Pioneers	16
Evelyn Dove	18
Winifred Atwell	20
Windrush and Beyond	22
Visual Arts	24
Film	26

Eni Aluko (Page 53)

Professor Christopher Jackson (Page 46)

CHAPTER 2: WHERE ARE ALL THE BLACK STEM HEROES?

The Surgeons	32
Activist Doctors	34
Groundbreaking Nurses	38
World Economist	42
Vaccine Developer	44
Modern Scientists	46

CHAPTER 3: SPORTS

Early Football Heroes	50
Women in Football	52
Boxing	54
Breaking Through as the Only One	56
Track Superstars	58
Paralympian Hero: Ade Adepitan	60

CHAPTER 4: THE HOME FRONT: POLITICS AND LAW

Community Activism	64
Everyday Heroes	68
Politics for the People	70
Public Platforms	72
Modern-day Givers	74

In Conclusion...	**76**
Glossary	**78**
Index	**79**

Dame Sharon White (Page 43)

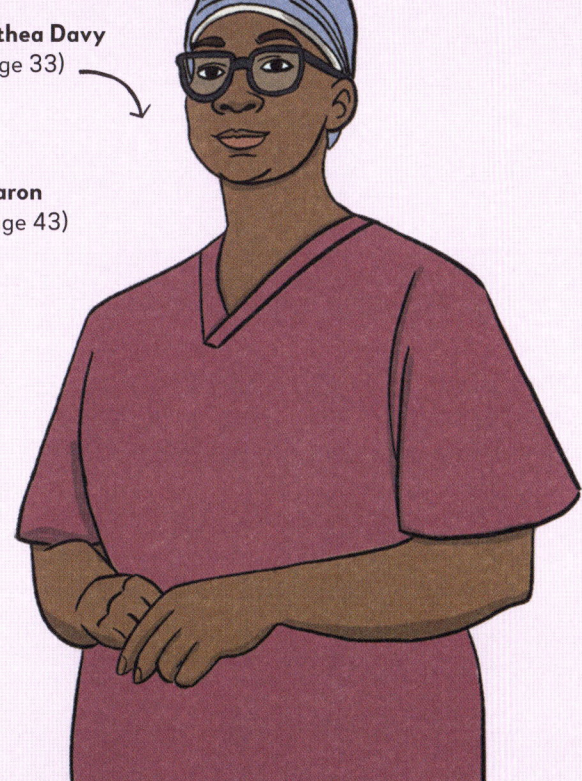

Anthea Davy (Page 33)

Timeline

In this book, you will meet amazing people from Black British history. This timeline shows some of them in order of when they were born, as well as some other key events from Black history.

MARY SEACOLE
23 Nov. 1805 Jamaica
Jamaican nurse and heroine of the Crimean War.

1805 **1863** **1873**

JAMES SAMUEL RISIEN RUSSELL
17 Sept. 1863 Guyana
One of the first Black British consultants and Professor of Medicine.

JOHN ALCINDOR
8 July 1873 Trinidad
Doctor and president of the African Progress Union.

CLAUDIA JONES
21 Feb. 1915 Trinidad
Journalist, activist, and founder of the Notting Hill Carnival.

WINIFRED ATWELL
27 Feb. 1914 Trinidad
First Black artist to sell one million records in the UK.

1915 **1914**

SIR WILLIAM ARTHUR LEWIS
23 Jan. 1915 St Lucia
Nobel Memorial Prize winner for Economics.

HARLEM RENAISSANCE
1920s-1930s
The Harlem Renaissance was an important period in African American music, dance, art, fashion, literature, theatre and politics, centred in Harlem, New York City in the US.

PRINCESS ADENRELE ADEMOLA
2 Jan. 1916 Nigeria
One of the earliest post-World War I nurses from Africa.

1916 **1917** **1920**

EARL CAMERON
8 Aug. 1917
Bermuda
One of Britain's first Black movie stars.

ALAN POWELL GOFFE
9 July 1920 London
Helped develop the Polio vaccine.

EMMA CLARKE
1876 Liverpool
First Black woman footballer in Britain.

ERNEST TRIMINGHAM
1880 Bermuda
Britain's first Black silent film actor.

DR HAROLD MOODY
8 Oct. 1882 Jamaica
Physician and civil rights activist.

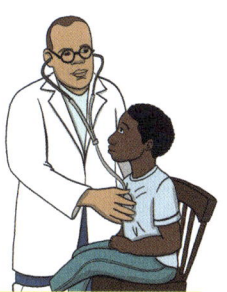

1876   1880   1882   1894

LEN BENKER JOHNSON
22 Oct. 1902 Manchester
Middleweight boxer and founder of the New International Society.

EVELYN DOVE
11 Jan. 1902 London
Black British musician and one of the first Black singers to appear on the BBC.

DR CECIL BELFIELD CLARKE
12 April 1894 Barbados
Physician and racial equality campaigner.

1902

THE SS *ROWAN* SINKING
9 Oct. 1921
A British passenger steamliner of the Laird Line which sank off the west coast of Scotland. Nine members of the Southern Syncopated Orchestra band lost their lives.

BERNIE GRANT
17 Feb. 1944 Guyana
Became one of the first Black MPs in 1987.

NEW INTERNATIONAL SOCIETY, 1946
Manchester
This was founded by Len Benker Johnson to counter racism, fascism, and class discrimination.

1921   1931   1944   1945   1946

LEAGUE OF COLOURED PEOPLES, 1931
Civil rights organisation founded in London by Harold Moody and other Black activists.

ALTHEIA JONES-LECOINTE
9 Jan. 1945 Trinidad
Scientist, central figure of British Black Panther Movement, and one of the Mangrove Nine.

7

OLIVE MORRIS
26 June 1952 Jamaica
Community activist and co-founder of the Brixton Black Women's Group.

THE *WEST INDIAN GAZETTE*, March 1958
Britain's first Black community newspaper, based in Brixton, London.

1948   **1952**   **1958**   **1959**

HMT *EMPIRE WINDRUSH*, 22 June 1948
The ship HMT *Empire Windrush* arrived at Tilbury. This is often thought of as the start of mass migration to Britain.

AN INDOOR CARIBBEAN CARNIVAL TAKES PLACE AT ST PANCRAS TOWN HALL, Jan. 1959
Organised by activist Claudia Jones, this event is believed to be the precursor to the Notting Hill Carnival.

1981   **1979**

BLACK CULTURAL ARCHIVES
1981 Brixton
This is the only national heritage centre dedicated to Black British history. It was founded by Len Garrison.

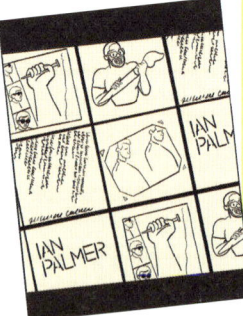

BLK ART GROUP
1979–mid-1980s This was a collective of Black British artists that formed in Wolverhampton. They challenged the inequalities that Black artists faced by exploring themes of Black British identity.

1985

BROADWATER FARM UPRISING, 6 Oct. 1985
This was a demonstration outside of a police station in Tottenham. The Black community were protesting over the death of Cynthia Jarrett the previous day.

BRISTOL BUS BOYCOTT
30 April 1963
The Bristol Omnibus Company refused to employ Black and Asian bus crews, so a group of activists boycotted the buses for four months. This led to the Race Relations Act in 1965.

CARIBBEAN ARTS MOVEMENT, 1966-1972
A group of Black artists, writers and poets that celebrated and promoted Caribbean arts in the UK.

1961   1963   1966

DONALD RODNEY
18 May 1961
Birmingham
Leading figure of the BLK Art Group in the 1980s.

NEW BEACON BOOKS OPENS, 1966
This is the UK's longest running bookshop dedicated to Black literature. It is based in North London and was founded by John La Rose.

THE UK GETS ITS FIRST BLACK PEER,
Learie Constantine (born 21 Sept. 1901).

1970   1969

MANGROVE NINE, 1970
A protest against police brutality in West London led to the wrongful arrest of Barbara Beese, Rupert Boyce, Frank Crichlow, Rhodan Gordon, Darcus Howe, Anthony Innis, Altheia Jones-LeCointe, Rothwell Kentish, and Godfrey Millett. These nine Black protesters successfully got themselves acquitted. Their trial was the first trial to publicly admit racial prejudice by the police.

DEATH OF GEORGE FLOYD
25 May 2020
The murder of George Floyd by a US police officer was filmed and shown worldwide, sparking an outcry and a resurgence of the Black Lives Matter movement – a racial justice movement. Black Lives Matter protests happened around the world, including in the UK.

2007   2020

LIVERPOOL INTERNATIONAL SLAVERY MUSEUM OPENS
23 Aug. 2007
This was the world's first museum dedicated to the legacy of the Transatlantic Slave Trade.

Foreword
by Sir Lewis Hamilton

Throughout my career, there have been many moments that fill me with pride, from crossing the finish line at the Abu Dhabi Grand Prix in 2020 to reach my seventh World Championship, to winning my 100th race in Russia in 2021. These achievements have been the outcome of the hard work and determination I put into racing every time I get into the car. However, despite the success I've had on the track, I've come to realise there's a more important job that needs to be done. I don't just want to be a champion on the track – I want to champion all the young people out there who don't think their dreams are possible.

Racing has been my passion since I was a kid, but there were times during my childhood when I lost confidence in my mission to truly succeed as a driver. I was one of the few Black students at my school and am now one of only a few Black employees within my industry. Throughout my career, I have used this difference to push myself further, but there have been times when I've felt the reality of being in a minority. It's during these times that I've taken my dad's advice to do my talking on the track. It's not always easy, but as I've grown older, I've become motivated to use my success as a platform to show all the young Black kids watching that their goals and aspirations are possible too. I want to show them that our community is resilient, and they can achieve their dreams if they believe in themselves.

As the only Black and working-class Formula 1 driver, my journey has often felt like a lonely one. However, I then remember the inspirational Black Britons who have walked lonely roads while shaping the future of our community, and I feel inspired to follow in their footsteps to support the next generation.

From Claudia Jones, who founded the Notting Hill Carnival, and pioneering nurse practitioner Mary Seacole, to prolific author and sociologist Stuart Hall and Harry Edward, Britain's first ever Black Olympian, we all stand on the shoulders of those who came before us. We're supported by their legacies, their sacrifices, and their commitment to help shape a better future for everyone.

Recently, as I reflected on my journey and those of the influential Black Britons who have come before me, I realised I wanted my legacy to extend beyond racing. Looking at the lack of representation in the end-of-season photographs across Formula 1 was a turning point for me. In that moment, I decided I had to be proactive in my desire to achieve a better future for the next generation. I realised the platform that my achievements have granted me should also serve as a pathway for the next generation of talent within my industry and beyond.

Last year, I announced my new charitable foundation, Mission 44, to help support young people from different underrepresented groups to reach their full potential. This includes helping to break down barriers that Black kids face every day when trying to find their place in society. It is my hope that our work will provide a stepping stone for the next Black engineer, the next female CEO, or the next disabled race car driver to achieve their dreams.

As we continue to change and shape society, I want my legacy to shine through the lives of every young Black kid who was told they won't succeed. The path to equality is not smooth but, by working together, I know we can create a brighter and fairer future for us all.

Introduction

What exactly does it mean when we talk about a legacy? Who can leave one? Are they something people leave behind when they die, or are legacies also being left now by people who are still living their lives?

Maya Angelou famously said:

"If you're going to live, leave a legacy. Make a mark on the world that can't be erased."

Maya is referring to people, their stories, and their actions leaving something behind for the world to see. So how did all the people that didn't have cameras, phones, and the internet to document and spread their greatness leave their mark on the world?

This book will unpick some of the history behind a few great Black British icons over the last 100 years or so. Some of these icons are not as well-known as they should be! This book is here to highlight how they have influenced life in the UK today and why it is important that they are not forgotten. Some of the influencers we will talk about lived way before the internet could make anything viral...

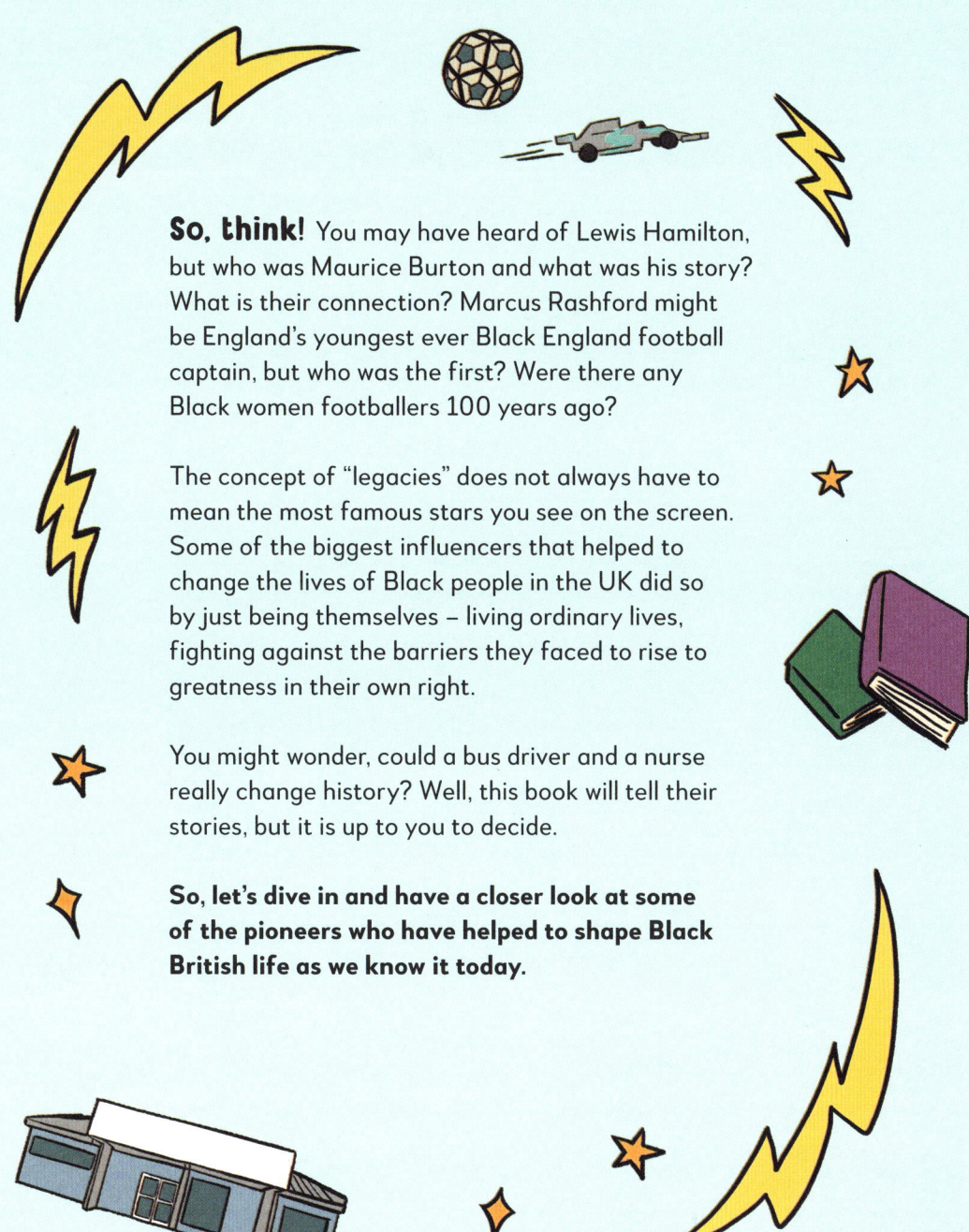

So, think! You may have heard of Lewis Hamilton, but who was Maurice Burton and what was his story? What is their connection? Marcus Rashford might be England's youngest ever Black England football captain, but who was the first? Were there any Black women footballers 100 years ago?

The concept of "legacies" does not always have to mean the most famous stars you see on the screen. Some of the biggest influencers that helped to change the lives of Black people in the UK did so by just being themselves – living ordinary lives, fighting against the barriers they faced to rise to greatness in their own right.

You might wonder, could a bus driver and a nurse really change history? Well, this book will tell their stories, but it is up to you to decide.

So, let's dive in and have a closer look at some of the pioneers who have helped to shape Black British life as we know it today.

Artists and Musicians

From modern genres like drill and grime to lovers rock back in the 1970s and 80s, jazz singers of the 1930s and 40s to the current music stars taking the world by storm, there are so many Black British contributions to art and music to celebrate. This chapter will look at some of the artistic talents that have left their mark on cultural life in the UK, starting with the early part of the 20th century.

Early Jazz Pioneers

When World War I ended in 1918, some of the Black soldiers who had come to Europe to fight remained in the UK. Their military skill was not the only legacy they left behind. They also influenced the music scene in the UK.

Harlem in New York City, USA, was a centre of the jazz scene in the 1920s.

Jazz music was becoming popular in the USA with the Harlem Renaissance in full swing, however, little is known about the UK and its own jazz scene. This new style of Black music changed the way British people danced and listened to music.

The jazz scene paved the way for freer and faster movements in both dancing and music.

In 1919, some Black soldiers from the West Indies, America, and Africa formed a jazz band called the Southern Syncopated Orchestra (SSO). This was the first Black British jazz band; really, the first Black British pop music band, because jazz was pop then! They played around the UK and Europe from 1919-1921. They were so popular that they were invited to play at Buckingham Palace for King George V. They played to all-white audiences, some of whom may not have seen a real Black band before, as blackface performances (when a white person paints their face to mockingly imitate a Black person) were common in music halls across the country. As a real Black band, the SSO changed the way white audiences saw Black performers.

The Southern Syncopated Orchestra performed at Buckingham Palace for King George V in 1919.

Sadly, in 1921, the SS *Rowan* – a ship carrying the band from Glasgow to Dublin – sank and nine band members drowned. The band stopped performing soon after, which was a huge loss for the jazz music scene. It is interesting to think of what could have happened if the ship hadn't sunk. What we know for sure is they were the first Black band to really put Black music on the map in the UK.

Evelyn Dove

The surviving members of the Southern Syncopated Orchestra went their separate ways. Let's take a look at one particular member – the fabulous Evelyn Dove. She had sung with the SSO and was seen as Britain's very own Josephine Baker (a popular American performer).

Evelyn Dove performing onstage.

Born in London in 1902 to a lawyer from Sierra Leone and an English mother, Evelyn studied at the Royal Academy of Music training in classical piano and singing. Life was tough back in those days, and racial discrimination stopped her classical music career ambitions. With the arrival of jazz, Evelyn met more Black musicians and was able to join the Southern Syncopated Orchestra and Chocolate Kiddies (another Black jazz band). Evelyn travelled all over the world singing to a variety of audiences much like current popstars do today.

Evelyn Dove, Elisabeth Welch, and Adelaide Hall were globally-recognised stars.

She was also in good company, too. Other Black singers like Elisabeth Welch and Adelaide Hall also performed this new popular style of music. Elisabeth and Adelaide were African American singers who settled in the UK in the 1930s. All three women sang jazz to packed-out concert halls all over Europe, which shows us the incredible popularity of their music at the time. They became some of the first international Black pop stars – the first of many talented Black singers who have been recognised across the globe.

Evelyn Dove became so popular in the UK that during World War II, she was given a regular BBC radio show alongside the Trinidadian singer Edric Connor. Evelyn continued singing on the BBC until 1949.

Sadly, she faded from stardom, and when she died in 1987, no one remembered her importance as one of the foremost Black singers of her time.

Hopefully this little insight into her life will help us to remember her legacy, and maybe you can sing a song in her name...

Evelyn Dove performed at the BBC until 1949.

19

Winifred Atwell

Winifred Atwell came to Britain from Trinidad to study at the Royal Academy of Music in 1946. She excelled in piano and was the first female musician to achieve the highest grading for musicianship.

Winifred played a newer sound called ragtime and boogie-woogie, a type of jazz music that became popular in the early 1950s. Winifred was one of the first Black faces to be seen on early TV screens and had a total of three number one hit singles – a first for any Black musician in the UK. Like the Southern Syncopated Orchestra and Evelyn Dove, she travelled the world singing and performing.

Winifred Atwell outside her salon.

Winifred also had other skills under her belt. She was a trained pharmacist and entrepreneur, and opened the first Black hair salon in Brixton in 1956, which deserves its own special mention, as Black hair most definitely matters!

Hair salons like the one Winifred opened are important for the community and for Black women all over the UK.

If we fast forward to today, musicians that play piano and sing include the British rapper and pianist Dave, and American artists Stevie Wonder and Alicia Keys. We can't help but think of all the talent that came before them and all the talent that is still to come.

Can you think of any other singers that play piano in their performances?

Stevie Wonder

Alicia Keys

Windrush and Beyond

The pace of the musical landscape quickened post-Windrush, with a new generation bringing a whole new sound and feel from the Caribbean to the UK music scene.

Calypso was brought over by Trinidadian artists such as Lord Kitchener and Edric Connor. Their lyrics were about their first-hand experience of living in the UK and the issues that Black people faced. This Caribbean influence on the music scene helped to start Britain's first Caribbean Carnival in 1959. This hoped to bring people together to fight racial tension (much more is written in The Black Curriculum's Carnival zine).

Lord Kitchener wrote songs about politics and the social inequalities Black people faced. Modern rappers and dub poets like Linton Kwesi Johnson, Akala, and Benjamin Zephaniah do the same thing today.

"London is the place for me."
Lord Kitchener, 1948

By the 1990s and the 2000s, the uniqueness of Black British music helped to create genres like jungle, drum and bass, house, garage, grime, and drill. Dizzee Rascal, Skepta, Arlo Parks, Jorja Smith, and Stormzy are now superstars, seen by millions worldwide. It's crazy to think that in such a short time, Black music in Britain has reached the heights it has today. Would Evelyn Dove ever have thought Black British music would become so popular?

Arlo Parks won the Mercury Award in 2021.
Jorja Smith won her second Brit Award in 2019.
Stormzy headlined at Glastonbury in 2019.

What do you think Evelyn Dove would think of the Black British music scene today?

Visual Arts

Ronald Moody was born in Jamaica in 1900. His early works from the 1930s are held by the Tate archive and he is one of the first Black British artists to exhibit internationally.

Moody arrived in Britain in 1923 to study dentistry at King's College London, but he decided to become a sculptor after viewing some sculptures at the British Museum. Ronald came from a high-achieving family – his brother Harold was a doctor and justice campaigner, and his other brother Ludlow was a physiologist and bacteriologist. All three brothers went to study at King's College London at a time when very few Black people went to university in Britain, let alone gained medical degrees at the highest of levels.

Ronald Moody sculpting in his studio.

By the 1950s and 1960s, more visual artists and writers arrived from the Commonwealth countries of Africa and the Caribbean. Ronald Moody's contemporaries (that's people alive at the same time as him) included Frank Bowling, the first Black Royal Academician; writer C.L.R. James; poet James Berry; textile designer Althea McNish; and many more. At that time it was difficult for Black creatives to get the recognition they deserved. The Caribbean Artists Movement was started in 1966, and Ronald Moody was one of its founding members. Its aim was to celebrate Caribbean identity and help artists share their ideas.

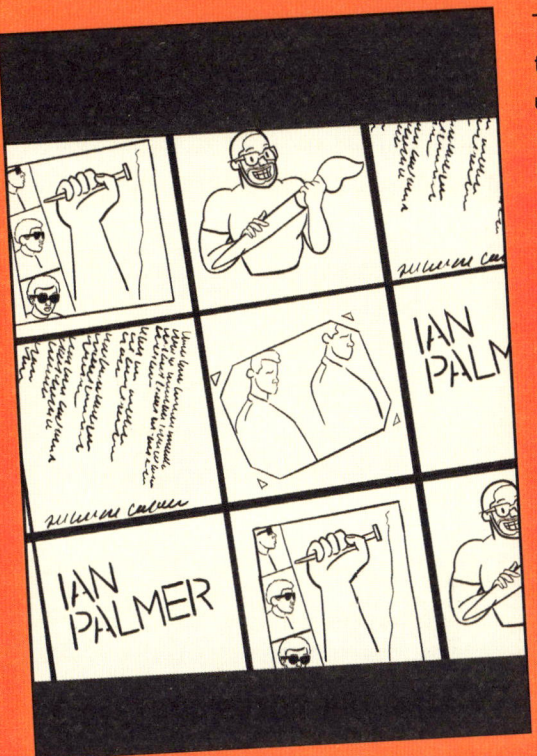

This gathering of Black creative talent from the Windrush era helped to maintain Black unity and solidarity despite the barriers they faced. They organised their own exhibitions, held gatherings, published their own newspapers, and created a legacy that later inspired Britain's BLK Art Group of the 1980s. The BLK Art Group included artists Keith Piper, Sonia Boyce, Lubaina Himid and Donald Rodney. This group of young Black artists were the first generation born from parents who had recently migrated to the UK.

The BLK Art Group focused on being Black and British, as they were the first generation born in the UK post-Windrush.

A poster for an exhibition by the BLK Art Group in Wolverhampton.

Donald Rodney, one of the founder members of the BLK Art Group, was born in 1961 in Birmingham. He was diagnosed with sickle cell anaemia, a genetic blood disease. He used art to explore themes of identity, racism, and illness to comment on society and politics. Donald Rodney created art in the 1980s, at a time when many Black British people were experiencing racial discrimination in housing, jobs, and education.

Donald Rodney died in 1998, at only 36 years old. Some of his works are now kept by the Tate gallery, maybe even keeping Ronald Moody's sculptures company.

Donald Rodney drawing in his sketchbook.

Film

In recent years, we've seen an explosion of Black British talent in the film world. Actors Idris Elba, Daniel Kaluuya, and John Boyega; writer, actor, and director Michaela Coel; and filmmakers Steve McQueen and Amma Asante have all won awards for their work. Not so long ago it might have been a distant dream for a Black person to receive such fame and even win an award.

Daniel Kaluuya won the Academy Award and the Golden Globe for Best Supporting Actor in 2021.

Amma Asante has won multiple awards at film festivals, including Best Feature at the Washington DC Filmfest in 2014.

John Boyega won Best Supporting Actor at the Golden Globes and the Critics' Choice Television Award in 2021.

Ernest Trimingham

One of the first Black British film actors was Ernest Trimingham. He was a silent movie and theatre actor born way back in 1880 (not long after the telephone was invented). Ernest came from Bermuda (a Caribbean island) and hoped to become famous in the UK.

He wrote and staged one of the very first Black-themed musicals at the Theatre Royal in Manchester called *Lily of Bermuda* in 1909. He went on to become one of the first Black actors in a British film, in *Dick Turpin: King of the Highwaymen* in 1912. He played a character called Beetles.

In 1919, Ernest Trimingham was in a Western movie called *Jack, Sam, and Pete*. He played a cowboy named Pete.

Rumour has it that in the 1940s, Ernest was in the same West End theatre as another Black film star from Bermuda: Earl Cameron...

Earl Cameron

In the 1950s, an actor named Earl Cameron was a prolific Black British movie star. Earl came to Britain from Bermuda in 1939. He started working in theatre before getting his big break in 1951 with a film called *Pool of London*. This film was a crime thriller, that also showed a romance between a Black man and a white woman, which was very rare to see on-screen in those days.

Earl Cameron played the character Pinder in the James Bond film *Thunderball* in 1965.

Although Earl Cameron may have been more famous than Ernest Trimingham, he still never quite managed to get the recognition he deserved. Acting in the 1950s and 60s, Earl faced huge challenges as there were very few parts written for Black actors. He wasn't famous in the same way that current stars are today.

Even so, he starred in more than 40 feature films, including the James Bond film *Thunderball*. One of his last acting roles was in 2010, when he had a small part in the film *Inception* with Leonardo DiCaprio, meaning he was still acting in his 90s. **What a legend!**

Amazingly, Earl's career lasted well over 60 years, and he was awarded a CBE (Commander of the Order of the British Empire) in 2009 for his services to film. In 2020, at the age of 102, Earl died peacefully in his sleep in England. His long life saw many changes for Black people both behind and in front of the camera. Although he did not receive an Oscar or BAFTA award himself, he paved the way for others after him – a true influencer.

Earl with his CBE medal in 2009.

"Where Are All the Black STEM Heroes?"

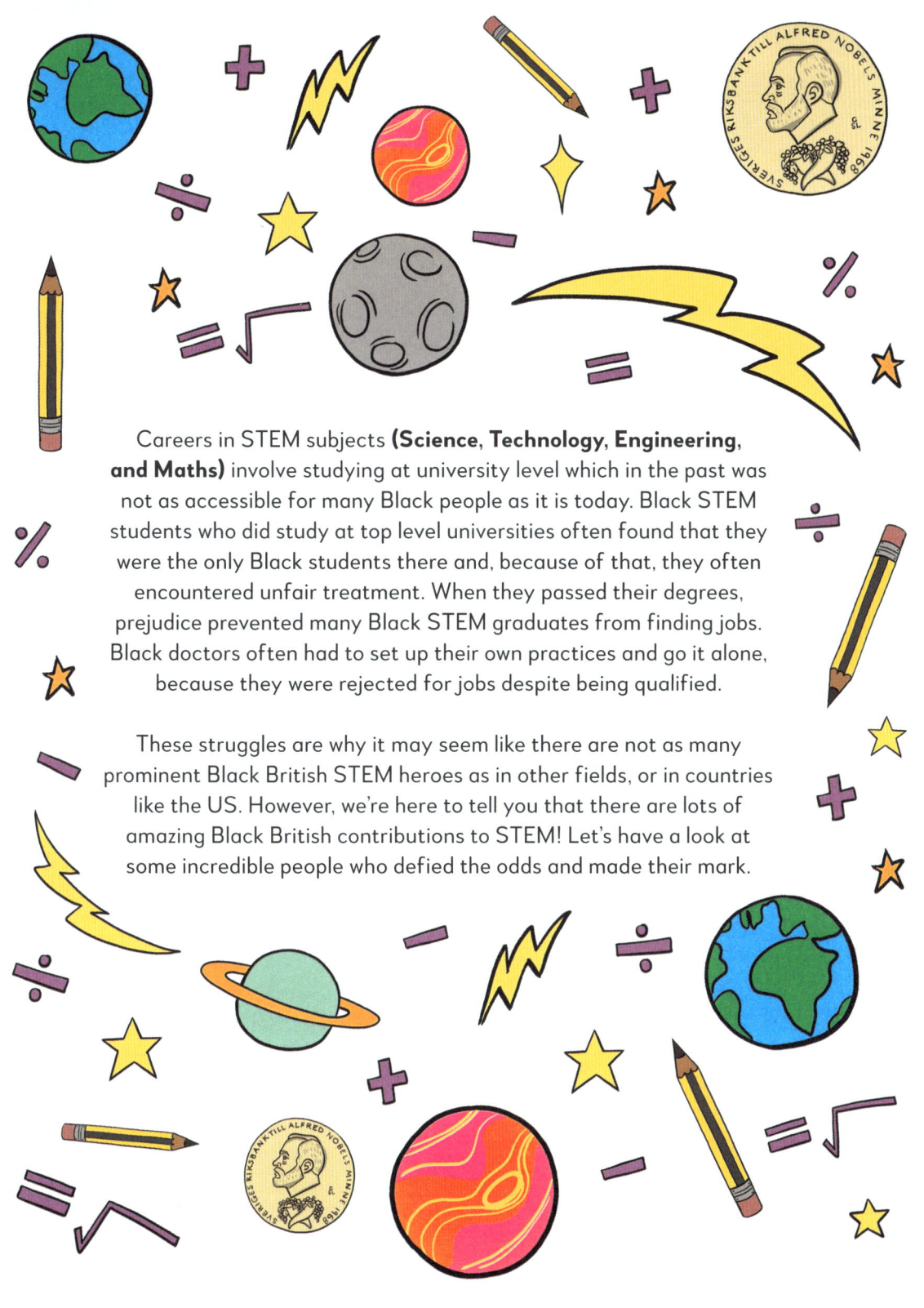

Careers in STEM subjects **(Science, Technology, Engineering, and Maths)** involve studying at university level which in the past was not as accessible for many Black people as it is today. Black STEM students who did study at top level universities often found that they were the only Black students there and, because of that, they often encountered unfair treatment. When they passed their degrees, prejudice prevented many Black STEM graduates from finding jobs. Black doctors often had to set up their own practices and go it alone, because they were rejected for jobs despite being qualified.

These struggles are why it may seem like there are not as many prominent Black British STEM heroes as in other fields, or in countries like the US. However, we're here to tell you that there are lots of amazing Black British contributions to STEM! Let's have a look at some incredible people who defied the odds and made their mark.

The Surgeons

James Samuel Risien Russell was a neurologist (nerve and brain specialist) who was born in Guyana in the Caribbean in 1863, more than 150 years ago. His father was Scottish, and his mother was of African heritage. He was sent to Scotland to complete his education in the 1880s. His talent for medicine led him to win a scholarship and trips to Paris and Berlin, before he eventually settled in London. He is credited as being one of the first Black consultant neurologists and was on the management board for the world's first school of neurology.

One area of expertise for Dr Russell was in the treatment of shell shock, a condition many soldiers developed during World War I. Shell shock caused tremors, shakes, headaches, and sensitivity to sounds and was similar to what we now call PTSD (post-traumatic stress disorder). By the early 1900s, Dr Russell had become a professor of medicine at UCL and set up his own upmarket central London practice, where he lived and worked for almost 40 years. He died very suddenly at his practice in 1939 in between seeing patients. His pioneering work is still referenced by medical students today, and you can now see a blue plaque outside his former practice at 44 Wimpole Street, London.

Dr James Samuel Risien Russell

DR J.S. RISIEN RUSSELL
1863–1939
Neurologist
lived and worked here from 1902

One of the first Black surgeons to be accepted as a fellow of the Royal College of Surgeons was Monica Lewin in 1962. Born in 1925 in Jamaica, Lewin received a scholarship to study at the Royal Free Hospital in London in 1944. She was credited as a trauma wound specialist.

Monica's inclusion as a fellow surgeon has opened the door for other Black women surgeons, including Samantha Tross, who became the first Black British female orthopaedic surgeon (that's a muscle and bone specialist) in 2005, and Anthea Davy in 2012.

Monica Lewin

Samantha Tross

Anthea Davy

The number of Black doctors and surgeons has increased since the early days of Dr James Samuel Risien Russell. However, the official figures suggest there's still room for a lot more. So now Stormzy is funding scholarships, we hope to see many more in the future. Who knows – maybe you might be one of them!

Activist Doctors

Doctors rarely have the reputation of being radical or outspoken, and they are often portrayed as mild-mannered and level-headed on TV or in movies. However, the UK has seen doctors that not only cared for the sick, but fought for change and equal rights.

John Alcindor

John Alcindor worked with the Red Cross during WWI at railway stations.

John Alcindor came to the UK from Trinidad. He graduated from Edinburgh University in 1899 and settled in London. During World War I, he wanted to use his training to help people. He applied to be a doctor in the army, but was rejected due to his race. Instead, he volunteered for the Red Cross, helping the wounded at railway stations as they returned home from war.

John was also a racial justice campaigner. He helped to arrange the first Pan-African Conference in 1900, which brought together international campaigners against racism. His medical research included looking at the links between poverty, poor diet, and poor health. John died in 1924, having no doubt inspired other medically trained activists.

Harold Moody

Earlier in this book, we mentioned the talented Moody brothers, Ronald, Ludlow, and Harold, who all studied scientific degrees at King's College London. Harold Moody was not only known for his skills as a doctor, but as a political campaigner for equal rights for Black people. The racial discrimination he experienced as a doctor denied him work in hospitals, so after he graduated, he set up his own private practice in Peckham. Like John Alcindor, he became an important part of his community. He set up the League for Coloured Peoples in 1931 and saved lives during the Blitz in World War II. He was in good company, as one of his colleagues in the League for Coloured Peoples was Dr Cecil Belfield Clarke, a brilliant doctor and activist with a secret that he kept for most of his life...

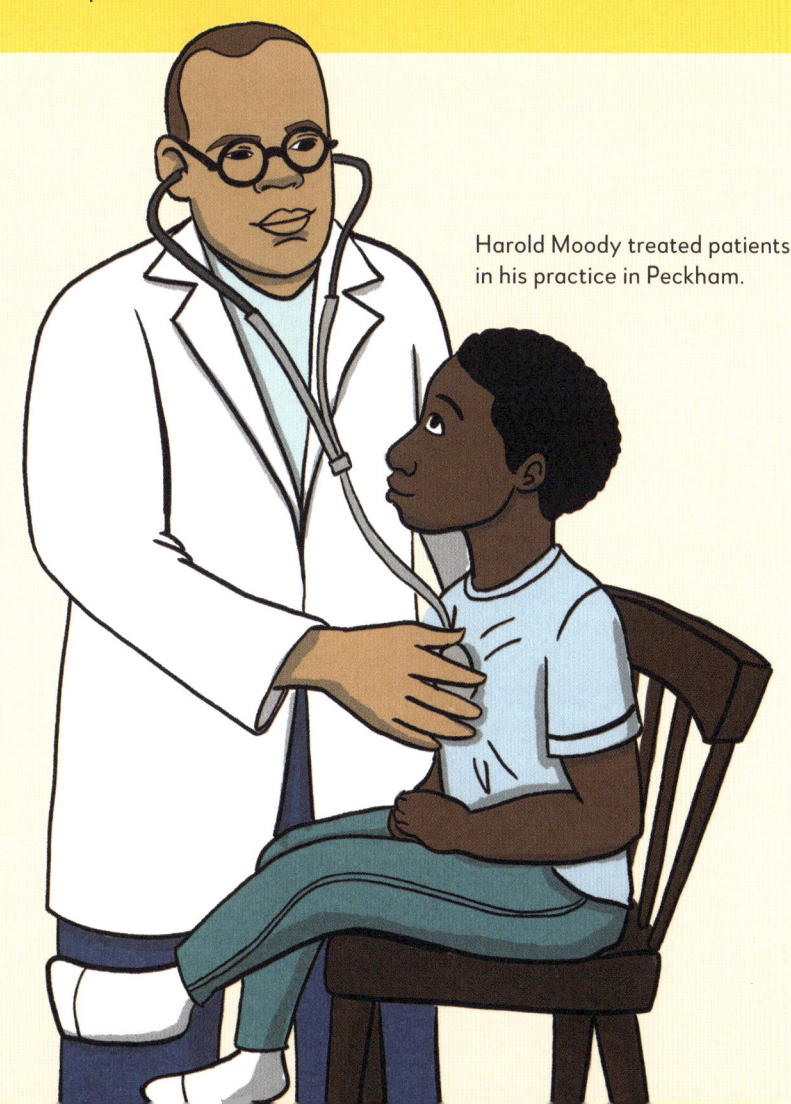

Harold Moody treated patients in his practice in Peckham.

Dr Cecil Belfield Clarke

Dr Cecil Belfield Clarke was a Black doctor who set up his own private practice in the London Borough of Southwark. Born in Barbados in 1894, Dr Clarke arrived in the UK in 1914 and studied at St Catharine's College, Cambridge University.

His impact on the college is still remembered today. Every year since 1952, the Belfield Clarke Prize has been awarded to the top student for outstanding performance in biological natural sciences.

Dr Clarke is famous for creating the "Clarke's Rule" which was the rule for the correct dosage of medicine for children aged 2-17. This uses a child's weight to work out the correct amount of medicine to give them. As well as his medical achievements, Dr Clarke was an activist and campaigner for civil rights. He was one of the founding members of the League of Coloured Peoples in 1931.

Dr Clarke was gay and lived with his partner for over 40 years. Their close friends knew about their relationship, but they had to keep it secret publicly, as relationships between two men were against the law until 1967 (three years before Dr Clarke died in 1970). Today, Dr Clarke is remembered as a pioneering doctor, a champion of racial equality, and a leading LGBTQIA+ figure. **Wow!**

Altheia Jones-LeCointe

Altheia Jones-LeCointe was another activist and scientist. She was born in Trinidad in 1945. Not only was she one of the famous Mangrove Nine, but she was also a leading member of the British Black Panther party, and a scientist. **Woah, a very busy lady!**

To read more about the Mangrove Nine, check out The Black Curriculum's resources online.

As a British Black Panther leader, she stood up for racial and social justice. She helped to organise a march in West London in 1970 against police brutality. She and eight others were arrested during the march. Their case became famous, and she and her fellow activists were known as the Mangrove Nine. Her academic gifts helped her to defend herself in a court of law and highlight the racial prejudice of the police at the time. She and the others were found not guilty and famously managed to get the courts to recognise that there was racial prejudice in society.

Altheia's scientific work often gets overlooked. She was a bioscientist, and after the Mangrove Nine case, she continued with her research on diabetes and sickle cell anaemia. All these brilliant doctors not only possessed extraordinary science skills, but courage and bravery in their commitment to their communities and their battle for racial equality and justice.

Groundbreaking Nurses

The British healthcare system underwent huge changes through the 19th and 20th centuries. Let's meet some of the nurses that made their mark during this time.

Mary Seacole

Mary Seacole is probably one of the best-known nurses in Black British history due to her work during the Crimean War. Her amazing achievements are recognised in the UK and worldwide. There have been many Black nurses after Seacole, particularly following the huge changes in the UK's health service in the years after World War II.

During the Crimean War, Mary Seacole set up the "British Hotel", a place where wounded soldiers could rest and recover.

Princess Adenrele Ademola

Princess Adenrele Ademola was a Nigerian nurse and princess born in 1916. She began her nursing career in the UK in 1937 training and working in various hospitals including Queen Charlotte's and Guy's Hospital in London. Princess Ademola's royal birth meant that she also attended many parties held by the Royal Family, combining not just royal duty, but service to the people.

She completed her midwife training in 1941. Her story was documented in a film entitled *Nurse Ademola* in 1944. Sadly, this film has since been lost, but some photographs of her in uniform remain.

Working 11 years before the NHS was established, Princess Ademola was one of the first Black nurses in Britain, and paved the way for many others in the future.

Constance Nelson and Monica Munroe

During World War II, huge numbers of people were involved in the war effort all over the world. British Commonwealth nurses were recruited to help in hospitals on the home front. Constance Nelson and Monica Munroe, pictured right, are part of a rich history of Black nurses coming to Britain to work. Many other Black nurses worked in the UK during the war and in the decades afterwards. After the war ended in 1945, 40,000 nurses came from Commonwealth countries to work in Britain.

Constance Nelson and Monica Munroe worked at Fulham hospital in 1945.

Dzagbele Matilda Asante

Kofoworola Abeni Pratt

The NHS was set up in 1948. Britain recruited many Commonwealth nurses to come over to train and work. This included Dzagbele Matilda Asante who started working in 1947, and Kofoworola Abeni Pratt, who started in 1950. Kofoworola Abeni Pratt was awarded the Florence Nightingale award in 1973 and became a fellow of the Royal College of Nursing in 1979.

Dame Elizabeth Anionwu

Dame Elizabeth Anionwu was born in Birmingham in 1947 and grew up dreaming of becoming a nurse. Her dream was realised when she became a nursing assistant at 16, eventually leading to a nursing career that focused on sickle cell disease. In 1979, she helped to set up the first specialist treatment centre for sickle cell in Willesden, London.

Her commitment to equality in healthcare led her to set up the Mary Seacole Centre for Nursing Practice in 1998. This pioneering centre had a mission to teach other nurses about illnesses, such as sickle cell disease, that particularly affect Black people. So great was Anionwu's expertise that she was given the title of "professor in nursing". She was also made a Dame in 2017.

Dame Elizabeth Anionwu received a Pride of Britain Award in 2019.

World Economist

Sir William Arthur Lewis was an economist (that's an expert on the wealth of a country). He was born in 1915 in St Lucia. He came to Britain in the 1930s to study at the London School of Economics. A brilliant learner, Lewis left school at 14 having completed his education two years early. He won a scholarship in 1932 and wanted to be an engineer at first, but was discouraged due to the lack of future job opportunities for Black engineers.

He decided to study a commerce degree, not knowing what economics was at first. He excelled in the subject however, gaining a first class degree and another scholarship, this time to do a PhD. He was one of the first Black lecturers in Britain and eventually became a professor in 1948 at the young age of 33. His brilliance in the field led him to develop new ideas and theories, including the "Lewis model" in 1954.

Sir William Arthur Lewis became a professor in 1948.

The Lewis model looked at the economics of developing countries and the relationship between the growth of wealth and the workers in these countries. As one of the leading Black economists in his field, Lewis was knighted in 1963. In 1979, he was awarded the Nobel Prize for Economic Sciences for his amazing work and became one of the first Black professors at Princeton University. Sir Lewis died in 1991 at the age of 76.

Nobel Prize Coin

Speaking of the name "Lewis", this brings us to another figure in the world of business and economics: Dame Sharon White, who is the chair of the John Lewis Partnership. She is an economist who became head of the famous company in 2020. She was the very first Black person to do so since the company started. Considering it started in 1864, that's a very long time!

Dame Sharon White with her Dame medal.

Vaccine Developer

Vaccine development has been essential for human survival. Vaccines allow us to bring infectious diseases under control or even get rid of them. Alan Powell Goffe was a specialist doctor whose work gave us vaccines against measles and polio in the 1940s. Sadly, not many people know about this brilliant man.

Alan Powell Goffe was born in 1920 to a Jamaican father and white English mother. He graduated with a medical degree from University College Hospital in 1944 and specialised in pathology (the study of diseases). He become Chief Medical Virologist (a virus specialist) in 1955 for the Wellcome Laboratories. His pioneering work helped develop vaccines for polio and measles, two of the most deadly childhood diseases at the time.

His career was sadly cut short when he died in a sailing accident at 46 years old. We will never know what he might have gone on to achieve, but his pioneering research and methods are still present to this day.

Modern Scientists

Black British STEM heroes are still making waves today. Some Black American names might be more well-known, such as Mae Jemison, the first Black woman in space; Katherine Johnson, the mathematician whose calculations helped the USA win the space race; and Dr Gladys West, who helped invent GPS. But, Britain has plenty of its own STEM heroes – let's meet some of them!

Dr Nira Chamberlain

Dr Nira Chamberlain is a Black mathematician and president of the Institute of Mathematics and its Applications. He was voted the "world's most interesting mathematician" in 2018 for his particular interest in mathematical solutions for industry. He is known for his ability to make maths interesting and has even invented his own long multiplication method.

Professor Christopher Jackson

Professor Christopher Jackson is a geologist (a scientist who studies the Earth). In 2020, he was the first Black presenter of a Royal Institution Christmas lecture in its entire 200-year history. His research takes him around the world, and he focuses on climate change and sustainability.

Dr Anne-Marie Imafidon

Dr Anne-Marie Imafidon is a maths and computing genius. After passing an A-level in computing at the age of 11, she was accepted into the University of Oxford and started studying for her degree at the age of 15. She gained a Master's degree in Mathematics and Computer Science by the time she was 20. Dr Anne-Marie now encourages other girls to take up STEM subjects with her company, Stemettes. She also co-presents the quiz show *Countdown*.

Dr Maggie Ebunoluwa Aderin-Pocock

Dr Maggie Ebunoluwa Aderin-Pocock is one of the UK's most famous space scientists. Maggie was born in London to Nigerian parents in 1968, one year before the first man landed on the Moon. Space was her lifelong inspiration. Her determination and passion led her to get a degree in Physics and a PhD in Mechanical Engineering. She is a specialist in telescope and satellite systems, as well as a television presenter, inspiring the nation to look up at the skies.

Sports

Black British people have been achieving amazing things in the world of sport for a long time. If we look at football today, we have fully integrated teams with players of all races. Many players make a statement against racism in football by taking the knee before games. There are also a huge number of Black sports personalities who are household names. We might wonder if things have always been this way, and if not, who came first? In this chapter, we will take a look at some of the early pioneers in the world of sport.

Early Football Heroes

Walter Tull, Arthur Wharton, and Andrew Watson have one thing in common: all three were early pioneers of a Black footballing tradition, playing in the UK over 100 years ago.

Walter Tull is remembered as one of the first Black players in the football league. He was also the first Black British officer in World War I. Before him, Andrew Watson was the first association footballer to play football at international level in the 1880s. And Arthur Wharton is believed to be the first Black professional football player ever! He played for Preston North End, reaching the FA Cup semi-finals in 1886.

Walter Tull

Andrew Watson

Arthur Wharton

So there have been Black football stars in the UK as long as the league itself has existed. Over the years, we've seen many barriers broken in football. Viv Anderson was one of the first Black players to have three lions on his shirt, playing for the men's senior England squad in 1978. At that time, Black footballers were often the target of intense racism, and Viv was one of only a few Black players to reach that level of international fame. It took another 15 years before England had their first Black captain, Paul Ince. Now there are several Black players representing England at the highest levels, such as Marcus Rashford and Bukayo Saka.

Viv Anderson made his debut for England in 1978 playing against Czechoslovakia.

Now there are several Black players representing England at the highest level. How many Black England players can you name that are playing today?

Bukayo Saka, England and Arsenal FC footballer.

Women in Football

In recent years, we have seen an increase in women taking up football. The history of women in the sport is interesting. Let's take a look at the story of early footballing legend, Emma Clarke, the first Black female professional football player.

Born in Liverpool in 1876, Emma was one of 14 children. She learned to play football while also working as an assistant in a sweet shop. She played in 1894 for the newly formed British Ladies, one of the first women's association club teams.

The club was formed to promote women in sport. It really was a game changer, as it was rare for women to play football back then. Not only was Emma one of the first Black women to play football, but she was part of the first women's team in the UK.

Emma and her teammates toured the UK playing at prestigious stadiums like Wembley. Emma is honoured with a blue plaque at the home of London's Crouch End team. She died in 1905.

In 1921, 16 years after her death, the football association decided it did not agree with women playing the sport. All women were banned from playing professionally between 1921 and 1971.

Alex Scott (middle) celebrating Arsenal's 14th Women's FA Cup win.

Today we can switch on the TV and see Alex Scott and Eni Aluko, who played for England before becoming football pundits. It's amazing to think of Emma and her teammates in the British Ladies playing 100 years before them.

I wonder what they would think seeing the Women's Super League on TV now?

Eni Aluko celebrating Chelsea's win in the Women's Super League in 2018.

Boxing

Although football had its issues with racism, Black players were at least allowed to play in mixed teams and could be named as champions. The same was not true about boxing, which had a colour bar in place.

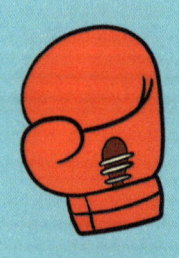

Anthony Joshua

Nicola Adams

There have been quite a few famous Black British boxers, including Frank Bruno, Lennox Lewis, Audley Harrison, Anthony Joshua, and Nicola Adams. However, Black boxers were subjected to a colour bar from 1911-1948. This meant that, even though they might win fights against white boxers, they were not allowed to be called British champions.

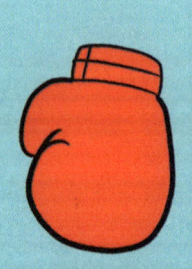

Len Benker Johnson fighting in the boxing ring.

Len Benker Johnson was the "unofficial" British boxing champion of 1926. He was not allowed to be credited as champion due to his skin colour. Only the children of white parents were allowed to gain the title of champion in boxing. Len was born in Manchester in 1902 and was subjected to lots of racial discrimination, including being refused a drink at his local pub. He was a talented boxer with 95 recorded wins out of 135 fights (although numbers can vary).

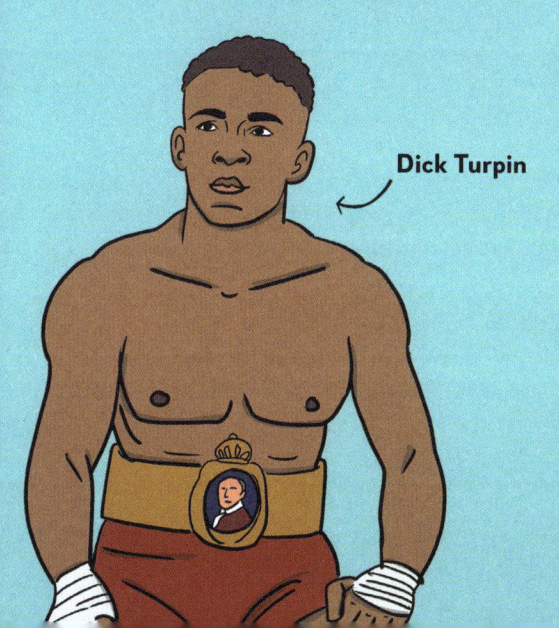

After he retired in 1933, he turned his attention to politics and became a trade union activist. He helped to create the New International Society in 1946, which was set up to fight far-right racist groups. He also became a friend of the Black American actor and singer Paul Robeson. Perhaps his energy for racial justice was fuelled by his fighting spirit. **What do you think he would think of the boxing champions of today?**

Once the colour bar was lifted, **Dick Turpin** became the first Black boxer to be named British champion in 1948. Len Johnson died in 1974, so in his lifetime he would have finally seen Black boxers become the champions they deserved to be.

Dick Turpin

Breaking Through as the Only One

There is much more Black representation in UK sport these days. You might remember the intro to this book mentioned a man called Maurice Burton, and a link to Sir Lewis Hamilton. Let's unpick that now.

Maurice Burton was Britain's first and only Black professional cyclist in the 1960s. Just like Sir Lewis Hamilton, Maurice was trying to break into a sport that had been traditionally seen as white. Lewis Hamilton is still the only Black professional Formula 1 driver. Maurice Burton was an incredible cyclist. At the age of 18 he became a national champion cyclist and was selected to go to the Commonwealth Games in New Zealand in 1974. But despite his efforts and early success, he was not chosen to represent the UK after 1974 and even received racist booing whilst picking up a trophy. Maurice decided that it would be easier to cycle in Belgium and so ended up moving there for the rest of his career. No doubt the level of racism he received had affected his career.

Maurice Burton cycling in the velodrome.

If we fast forward to today, Sir Lewis Hamilton is credited as one of the most successful Formula 1 drivers of all time. Born in 1985 in Hertfordshire with Grenadian and English heritage, Lewis showed a talent for racing at an early age. He started track racing in the early 1990s and won his first competition aged 10.

Supported by his father, who took him to all his early races, Lewis Hamilton's skills and talent helped him to sign with McLaren in 2007. He is the first and only Black person ever to race in Formula 1. Despite receiving his fair share of racism and unfair treatment, his steely determination has helped him use his platform to fight for racial equality in the sport. With more than 100 wins, he is a world champion, record holder, and a true Black British hero.

Hamilton celebrating his 7th World Championship.

Track Superstars

Black athletes are now a consistent presence on the podium at the Olympics, and Linford Christie, Dame Kelly Holmes, and Denise Lewis are household names. However, this was not always the case.

Jack London running in the Olympics.

You might have heard of the Black American track and field athlete Jesse Owens, who famously won four gold medals at the 1936 Olympics. Harry Edward and Jack London were two Black British track and field athletes who came before him. Harry Edward won bronze in 1920, and Jack London won silver and bronze in 1928.

Harry Edward

Anita Neil

Tessa Sanderson

Women's contributions to sport have historically been overlooked. Anita Neil was the first Black British woman to compete in an Olympic event in 1968. Her presence was short lived, as a lack of funding for her training in track and field meant she had to retire at the age of 23.

Her teammates included Sonia Lannaman and Beverley Goddard, who went on to win the bronze in the 4 x 100 metre relay in Moscow in 1980. This was followed by Tessa Sanderson, who was the first Black British woman to win the gold in javelin in Los Angeles in 1984.

The 1980s proved to be an important decade in Black Olympic history. Daley Thompson won gold in 1980 and 1984 in the decathlon, one of the most gruelling track and field events. At one point, he was even named greatest athlete ever.

Daley Thompson doing the high jump.

There are 10 events in the decathlon at the Olympics. How many can you name?

Paralympian Hero: Ade Adepitan

One of the most famous presenters on TV is Ade Adepitan, a wheelchair user and former British basketball Paralympian.

He represented Britain in Athens in 2004 where he and his teammates picked up a bronze medal. Born in 1973 in Nigeria, Ade contracted a disease called polio when he was still an infant, which affected his legs.

Ade playing basketball for Team GB.

Ade has also written a series of books for children.

He moved to the UK at the age of three and grew up in East London. He started playing wheelchair basketball at age 12 and went on to compete at the Paralympics for Team GB. He was part of the team that won bronze at the 2004 Summer Paralympics, and gold at the 2005 Paralympic World Cup. Although he is now known as a TV presenter, it is important to recognise Ade's achievements not only in sport, but also in raising disability awareness.

The Home Front: Politics and Law

Black people have fought for equality over many years and across many fields and professions. One example is Una Marson, an activist and writer who arrived in the UK from Jamaica in 1932 and was dismayed by the colour bar. Together with Harold Moody, who had similar experiences of racism, she created the League of Coloured Peoples, a civil rights organisation. Una was a feminist, poet, and playwright, and her efforts to promote literature and education on racial issues in the UK was groundbreaking at the time. She was hired as a producer on the BBC radio show *Caribbean Voices* in the 1940s, making her the first Black woman broadcaster on the BBC.

Let's meet some more amazing pioneers of social justice...

Community Activism

Claudia Jones was originally from Trinidad, but moved to New York's Harlem at the age of eight years old. Her family didn't have much money, and her mother died when Claudia was 13 years old. Claudia believed her mother's death was caused by overwork. Claudia's tragic beginnings made her want to campaign for workers' rights and improve conditions for people. She became a member of the Communist Party in the United States. The Immigration and Nationality Act of 1952 allowed the US government to deport immigrants who spoke out against the status quo too much. Claudia was arrested, imprisoned, and deported from the United States. At the time, Trinidad was a Commonwealth country, so she was given the choice to go to either Trinidad or Britain. She chose Britain.

Claudia arrived in Britain in the 1950s and established herself in the Caribbean community. She helped to set up one of the first Black newspapers, *The West Indian Gazette*.

She is more famously known for her involvement in starting the Notting Hill Carnival. There was a lot of racial tension in the Notting Hill area of London during the 1950s. Claudia and her carnival crew were committed to bringing people together through Carnival celebrations.

Claudia's legacy still vibrates throughout the UK, with Caribbean carnivals happening in places all over Britain, including Luton, Leeds, and Bristol.

Olive Morris was a community activist from Brixton, London. As a young campaigner, Olive helped to start the Brixton Black Women's Group, which fought for Black women's rights. She also joined the British Black Panther party as a youth and was committed to raising awareness of injustices suffered by Black people. She campaigned against stop and search laws (sus laws), which unfairly targeted Black people. She is famous for occupying spaces in Brixton and setting them up as places where members of the community could seek help and support. This brave type of activism made such an impact on the Brixton community that a building was named after her: Olive Morris House. Her death in 1979 at the age of 27 was a tragic loss for the community, but her legacy lives on.

Brixton has been a hub for Black British people since the early days of the *Windrush*. Another famous activist operating in Brixton was **Pearl Alcock**, who was a champion of LGBTQIA+ rights. Pearl was born in 1934 and came to Britain in the 1950s. Recognising the need for a safe space for the Black LGBTQIA+ community to gather, Pearl set up basement bars (sometimes called shebeens) in the Brixton area. She was an artist, activist, and a true icon. She ran her basement bars right up to her death in 2006 at the age of 72.

Campaigner and youth worker **Sybil Phoenix** started Britain's first ever Black youth centre in Pagnell Street in Deptford. In the 1970s, she recognised that young Black people needed to have a safe space to go. Thanks to her work in the community, in 1973 she was also the first Black woman to receive an MBE. She remained strong even when her beloved youth centre was burned down in a racist attack. The centre was rebuilt in 1981 and renamed the Moonshot. She even bought a house that she dedicated to housing homeless women. This was called the Marsha Phoenix Memorial Trust, named after her daughter. Sybil's story might not be well-known, but she was an important figure that changed many people's everyday lives.

Dorothy Kuya was a teacher and campaigner from Liverpool. She successfully campaigned for the opening of the Liverpool International Slavery Museum, which was set up in 2007. She was also part of the organisation Teachers Against Racism. In April 2021, students of the University of Liverpool voted to name a hall of residence after her so her legacy is remembered by future generations.

Books by Black authors have not always been widely sold in general bookstores. Enter **Eric and Jessica Huntley,** a married couple from Guyana. Both were keen community activists who were determined to spread Black educational resources and help support Black parents to educate their children. They set up a publishing company and bookstore called Bogle-L'Ouverture Publications, which was dedicated to writing by Black authors.

Others joined the fight to tackle bias in the book world, too. Allison & Busby publishers was founded by Margaret Busby, one of Britain's first Black female publishers. Other Black-owned bookshops included New Beacon Books, which is still in North London to this day. These figures and their bookshops show how ordinary people working together can make big, lasting changes in society and their community.

Everyday Heroes

So far in this book we have read about politicians, sports heroes, pop stars, and scientists. But you don't need to be famous to have an impact on the world. The everyday experiences of ordinary people are incredibly important.

Joe Clough was a bus driver on route 11 in London.

Jamaican-born Joe Clough is noted as being London's first Black bus driver. In 1910, he joined the London General Omnibus Company driving the number 11 bus between Liverpool Street and Wormwood Scrubs. He moved to Bedford, Bedfordshire with his family just before World War I. During the war, he used his driving skills to serve as an ambulance driver on the front line.

After the war, he returned to driving buses in Bedford. He was once wrongfully sacked by a racist official for driving over the speed limit. However, a group of his fellow bus drivers stuck up for him, and he won his job back.

Although Joe's story happened in the early part of the 20th century, it feels similar to the Bristol bus drivers who fought against the colour bar in the 1960s. At the time, the Bristol Omnibus Company refused to employ Black or Asian drivers. An activist called Paul Stephenson led the Bristol Bus Boycott in 1963. He and his fellow activists refused to use buses for four months until the racist ban changed. Because of the campaign, the ban was lifted, and Black and Asian people could get jobs as bus drivers.

Paul Stephenson made an impact on people's lives and jobs through his activism.

Politics for the People

1987 was a big year in British politics, because the first four Black MPs were elected. One of them was Bernie Grant. He was born in 1944 and was the Labour MP for Tottenham until his death in 2000. Bernie had been a council leader during the Broadwater Farm Uprising in 1985, which was a response to the tragic death of Cynthia Jarrett who died of a heart attack whilst police searched her home. It was one of many uprisings that happened in the 1980s as a result of racism. During this time, Bernie spoke out against police brutality and other injustices that Black people faced. Bernie Grant was popular with the people of Tottenham because of how he spoke up for people and empowered others. He was such a popular local figure that the Bernie Grant Arts Centre was opened in Tottenham in 2007.

Before Bernie, another groundbreaking Black politician was David Pitt. He was born in Grenada and graduated from the University of Edinburgh. He was the first Black person to run as a Labour MP in 1959. This was a time of major racial tension in Britain, and David received death threats. However, he was determined to stand for election, which showed his bravery and commitment. He did not win in 1959, but that did not stop him wanting to enter politics and make a difference.

He became a London County Council member in 1961 and was the first Black chairman of the Greater London Council in 1974. He stood once more as MP in 1970 but lost. However, he was given a seat in the House of Lords in 1975 and named Baron Pitt of Hampstead.

David Pitt was named Baron Pitt of Hampstead in 1975.

It wasn't until 1987 that Britain saw its first Black MPs. We could say that David Pitt's commitment helped open the door for others to follow.

Diane Abbott

Like Bernie Grant, Diane Abbott was also elected as MP in 1987. She was the first Black woman to become an MP. She was born to Jamaican parents in the 1950s and later attended Cambridge University. She is one of the longest serving Black MPs ever, with a career lasting more than 35 years. As a Labour MP, Diane represents the borough of Hackney and Stoke Newington in London. Diane has opened the door for a whole host of other Black women in politics, including Dawn Butler and Marsha de Cordova. Her continued presence on the political scene has helped elevate different voices and change the face of British politics.

Public Platforms

Political advocates and campaigners don't always have to sit in the Houses of Parliament. Today, we see a number of young activists campaigning and fighting for change on social media and other platforms.

The rise of the Black Lives Matter movement has awakened a new desire for change. The power of social media means that we have a whole new way to fight injustice and inequality. Here are a few activists who are making waves...

Munroe Bergdorf

Munroe Bergdorf is a model and activist for race and trans rights in the UK. She famously spoke out about racism and was then dropped as a model for L'Oreal as her views at the time were deemed too controversial. In recent years, Munroe's outspoken and direct approach means she is recognised as a voice to be listened to.

Marcus Rashford

Marcus Rashford is not just a footballer, but a champion for social and racial equality. He famously campaigned for free school meals. He was also committed to encouraging all Premier League players to take the knee in recognition of Black Lives Matter. Rashford recognises the importance of taking a stand and has brought the issue of racism in football to the public's attention.

Lady Phyll

Lady Phyll is famous for starting UK Black Pride, an event to promote unity among the Black LGBTQIA+ community. Her dedication to promoting equality for all makes her a true icon.

Dr Shola Mos-Shogbamimu

Dr Shola Mos-Shogbamimu is a political commentator, lawyer, activist, and author. Her straight-talking approach is powerful and challenging. She is noted for championing social and racial justice and her strong advocacy for the Black community.

Nova Reid

Nova Reid is a public speaker and author of the book *The Good Ally*. Her activism and anti-racist work has led her to set up her own podcast to discuss racism and how to be anti-racist.

Modern-day Givers

Not all activism takes the form of podcasts, social media posts, and frontline campaigning. Activism can take the form of creation and donation.

Born in Croydon in 1993, Stormzy is well-known for being the first Black British solo artist to headline at Glastonbury in 2019.

#Merky Books publishes books for both adults and children.

But it is through Stormzy's generosity that we see a true activist in action. Stormzy has used his financial success to help others. He started his own publishing imprint, #Merky Books, which is dedicated to publishing books by diverse voices.

He also set up his own scholarship fund, the Stormzy Scholarship, which supports Black students at Cambridge University. Stormzy shows that activism can mean using your platform to help create opportunities for others.

The Stormzy Scholarship supports Black students at Cambridge University.

SCHOLARSHIP

IN CONCLUSION...

Recognising Black British people's contributions to UK history is **crucial** for **empowering** others. **Len Garrison** is the founder of the **Black Cultural Archives** in Brixton; the UK's first national Black heritage centre. The centre reminds us of the importance of recording and **celebrating** the achievements of Black people, and recognising their role in shaping the UK and the world.

Len's vision helped to create a dedicated centre for Black British history, and this book hopes to add its part to that legacy. We know there are still so many untold and unheard stories, more than we could fit into this book.

This book is intended to **kickstart your own exploration** into your local or family history. We hope you **tell us all about what you find out!**

YOU MIGHT EVEN WRITE YOUR OWN LEGACY BOOK ONE DAY!

77

Glossary

Activism
The use of direct action, for example boycotting something, to push for political or social change.

Boycott
Refusing to use or buy something from a company in order to protest something.

British Black Panther Party
A Black British organisation active in the 1960-70s that focused on Black empowerment and equal rights in the UK.

Civil rights
The principle that every person should be treated equally under law, regardless of who they are.

Colour bar
A system that prevented people of colour from accessing jobs, opportunities, and public spaces.

Commonwealth
A group of 56 countries that includes the UK and independent nations that were once colonies within the British Empire. The countries have no legal obligations to one another but do cooperate on economic and humanitarian matters.

Equality
Every person having the same rights and opportunities.

LGBTQIA+
An inclusive term that includes people across a wide range of genders and sexualities. It stands for **L**esbian, **G**ay, **B**isexual, **T**ransgender, **Q**ueer/**Q**uestioning, **I**ntersex, **A**sexual/**A**romantic.

MP
Member of Parliament elected to represent their local area in the House of Commons.

Pioneer
A person who starts something new and leads the way for others to follow.

Prejudice
An unfair and usually negative judgement towards an individual or group.

Racial discrimination
When people are treated unfairly because of their race.

Stereotype
A simplified belief about certain groups, often linked to race, culture, gender, age, or class.

Trade union
An organisation committed to protecting workers' rights.

You might notice that we capitalise the B in Black, but not the w in white. Here is The Black Curriculum's note on why this is:

We capitalise the B in Black because the word Black in this context reflects a shared sense of identity and, to a certain extent, a community. The case for capitalising Black is also rooted in humanising and uplifting groups that have historically been stripped of this right. White, in this context, does not suffer from the same historical happenings, especially in the context of Britain.

Index

A
Abbot, Diane 71
activists 34–37, 64–67, 72–75
actors 26–29
Ademola, Princess Adenrele 39
Adepitan, Ade 60–61
Aderin-Pocock, Dr Maggie Ebunoluwa 47
Akala 22
Alcindor, John 34
Alcock, Pearl 65
Aluko, Eni 53
Anderson, Viv 51
Anionwu, Dame Elizabeth 41
artists 24–25
Asante, Amma 26
Asante, Dzagbele Matilda 40
athletics 58–59
Atwell, Winifred 20–21

B
Bergdorf, Munroe 72
BLM (Black Lives Matter) 72
boxing 54–55
Boyega, John 26
British Black Panther party 37, 65
Burton, Maurice 56

C, D
Cameron, Earl 28–29
Chamberlain, Dr Nira 46
Clarke, Dr Cecil Belfield 35–36
Clarke, Emma 52
Clough, Joe 68
cycling 56
Davy, Anthea 33
doctors 24, 34–37
Dove, Evelyn 18–19

E, F, G
economists 42–43
Edward, Harry 58
film 26–28
football 50–53
Formula 1 57

Garrison, Len 76
Goffe, Alan Powell 44–45
Grant, Bernie 70

H
Hall, Adelaide 19
Hamilton, Sir Lewis 57
Huntley, Eric and Jessica 67

I, J, K
Imafidon, Dr Anne-Marie 47
Jackson, Professor Christopher 46
jazz 16–17, 20
Johnson, Len Benker 55
Jones, Claudia 64
Jones-LeCointe, Altheia 37
Joshua, Anthony 54
Kaluuya, Daniel 26
Kitchener, Lord 22
Kuya, Dorothy 66

L
League of Coloured Peoples 35, 36, 63
Lewin, Monica 33
Lewis, Sir William Arthur 42–43
LGBTQIA+ 36, 65, 73
London, Jack 58

M
Mangrove Nine 37
Marson, Una 63
medicine 32–35, 44–45
Moody, Harold 24, 35, 63
Moody, Ronald 24–25
Morris, Olive 65
Mos-Shogbamimu, Dr Shola 73
Munroe, Monica 40
music 16–23

N
Neil, Anita 59
Nelson, Constance 40
nurses 38–41

P
Paralympics 60–61
Parks, Arlo 23
Phoenix, Sybil 66
Phyll, Lady 73
Pitt, David 71
politicians 70–71
Pratt, Kofoworola Abeni 40

R
Rashford, Marcus 50, 72
Reid, Nova 73
Rodney, Donald 25
Russell, Dr James Samuel Risien 32

S
Saka, Bukayo 51
Sanderson, Tessa 59
Scott, Alex 53
Seacole, Mary 38–39
Smith, Jorja 23
Southern Syncopated Orchestra 17–18
Stephenson, Paul 69
Stormzy 23, 33, 74–75
surgeons 32–33

T, V
Thompson, Daley 59
Trimingham, Ernest 27
Tross, Samantha 33
Tull, Walter 50
Turpin, Dick 55
TV presenters 47, 60–61
vaccines 44–45

W
Watson, Andrew 50
Welch, Elizabeth 19
Wharton, Arthur 50
White, Dame Sharon 43
World War I 16, 32, 34, 50
World War II 19, 39–40
writers 61, 67, 73

Project Editor Rosie Peet
Project Art Editor Stefan Georgiou
Senior Acquisitions Editor Katy Flint
Managing Art Editor Vicky Short
Production Editor Siu Yin Chan
Production Controller Louise Minihane
Publishing Director Mark Searle

Written by Lania Narjee
Illustrated by Chanté Timothy

First published in Great Britain in 2022 by Dorling Kindersley Limited
DK, One Embassy Gardens, 8 Viaduct Gardens, London SW11 7BW

The authorised representative in the EEA is Dorling Kindersley Verlag GmbH. Arnulfstr. 124, 80636 Munich, Germany

Page design copyright © 2022 Dorling Kindersley Limited
A Penguin Random House Company

Artwork copyright © Chanté Timothy, 2022

Text copyright © The Black Curriculum CIC 2022

10 9 8 7 6 5 4 3 2
002–328148–Aug/2022

All rights reserved.
No part of this publication may be reproduced, stored in or introduced into a retrieval system, or transmitted, in any form, or by any means (electronic, mechanical, photocopying, recording, or otherwise), without the prior written permission of the copyright owner.

A CIP catalogue record for this book is available from the British Library.
ISBN: 978-0-2415-5281-0

Printed in the UK

The publisher would like to thank Chima Itabor for providing the authenticity read; Victoria Armstrong, Lisa Gillespie, and Julia March at DK for editorial support; and Ilhan Rayen Awed and Saffa Khalil at The Black Curriculum.

For the curious

www.dk.com

This book was made with Forest Stewardship Council ™ certified paper—one small step in DK's commitment to a sustainable future. For more information go to www.dk.com/our-green-pledge

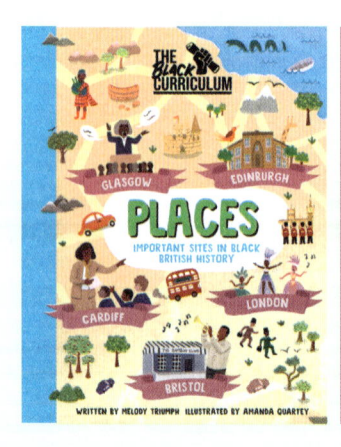

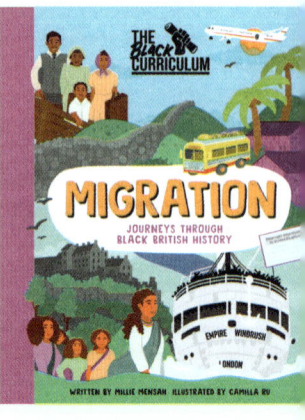

Want to find out more about Black British history? Go to **www.theblackcurriculum.com** to find videos, zines, classroom resources, and more.

If you've enjoyed this book, look out for the other books in this series! *Places: Important Sites in Black British History* and *Migration: Journeys Through Black British History.*

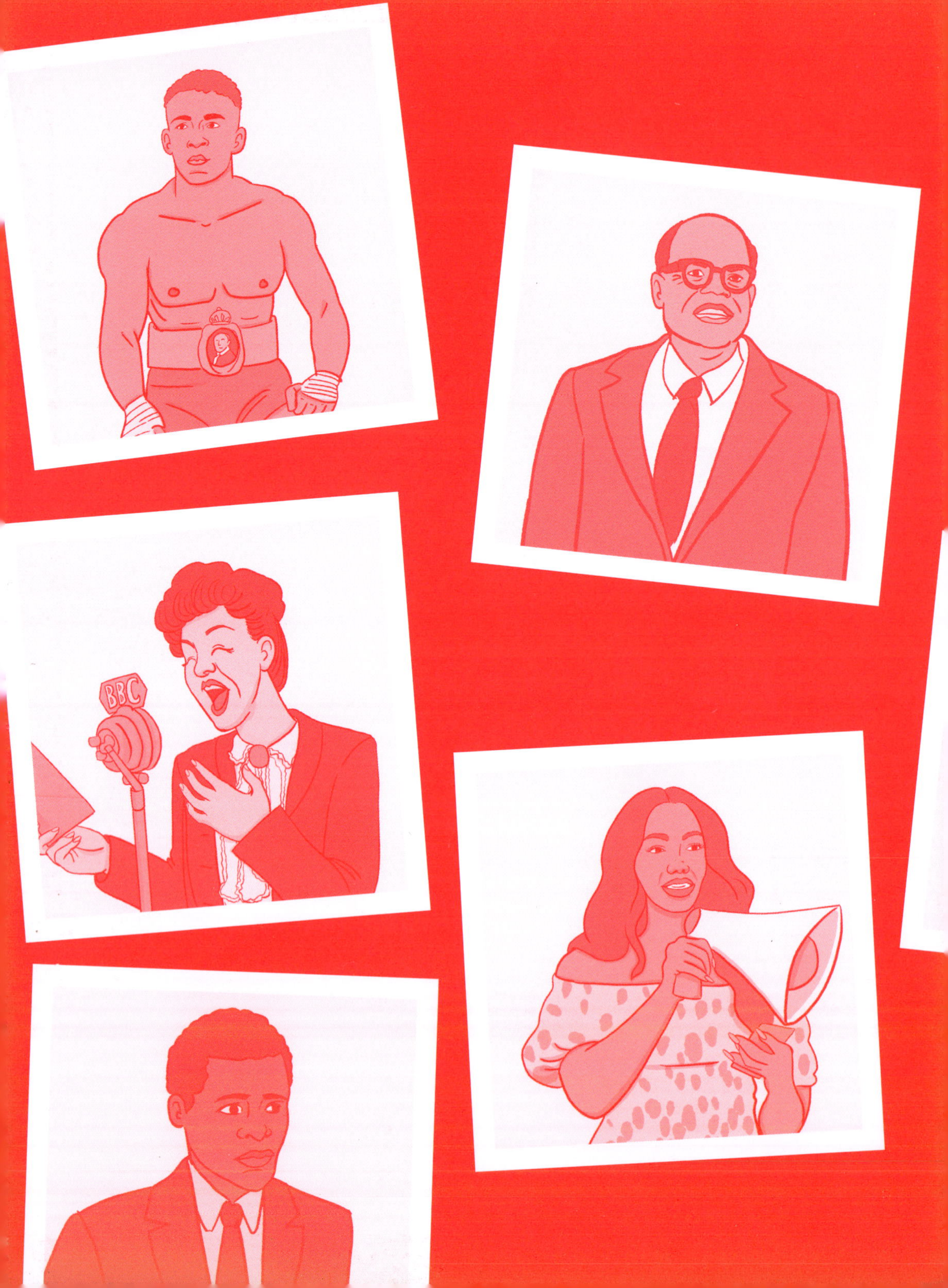
BBC